Pharaohs

by Grace Hansen

DISCOVERING ANCIENT EGYPT

Abdo Kids Jumbo is an Imprint of Abdo Kids
abdobooks.com

abdobooks.com

Published by Abdo Kids, a division of ABDO, P.O. Box 398166, Minneapolis, Minnesota 55439. Copyright © 2024 by Abdo Consulting Group, Inc. International copyrights reserved in all countries. No part of this book may be reproduced in any form without written permission from the publisher. Abdo Kids Jumbo™ is a trademark and logo of Abdo Kids.

Printed in the United States of America, North Mankato, Minnesota.

102023

012024

Photo Credits: Alamy, Getty Images, Shutterstock, ©Jeff Dahl p1/CC BY-SA 4.0

Production Contributors: Teddy Borth, Jennie Forsberg, Grace Hansen
Design Contributors: Victoria Bates, Candice Keimig

Library of Congress Control Number: 2023937692

Publisher's Cataloging-in-Publication Data

Names: Hansen, Grace, author.

Title: Pharaohs / by Grace Hansen

Description: Minneapolis, Minnesota : Abdo Kids, 2024 | Series: Discovering ancient Egypt | Includes online resources and index.

Identifiers: ISBN 9781098268466 (lib. bdg.) | ISBN 9781098269166 (ebook) | ISBN 9781098269517 (Read-to-Me ebook)

Subjects: LCSH: Pharaohs--Juvenile literature. | Kings and rulers, Ancient--Juvenile literature. | Royalty--Juvenile literature.

Classification: DDC 932--dc23

OCTOBER 2024

Table of Contents

Ultimate Rulers

Pharaohs were the ultimate

rulers of ancient Egypt. They

had a large amount of power.

5

Egyptians believed the pharaoh was the god Horus in human form. Horus was one of the most important gods.

Horus

The word *pharaoh* comes from the Egyptian *per 'aa*, meaning "great house." However, the ancient Egyptian rulers were not called pharaohs. They each had five names that made up their title.

9

The pharaoh was almost always male. He usually had many wives. One wife was especially important. Her sons were the next in line for the throne.

11

The earliest pharaohs owned all the land. Over time, pharaohs gave some of it to **temples**. They also gifted it to certain families.

13

Pharaoh Duties

The pharaoh's duties included **preserving** *ma'at*. This was the order and **harmony** of the universe. The pharaoh fought off enemies to keep away **chaos**.

15

The Afterlife

The pharaoh was considered a god even after death. Egyptians carefully **mummified** and buried the body. The body was buried with everything the pharaoh might need in the afterlife.

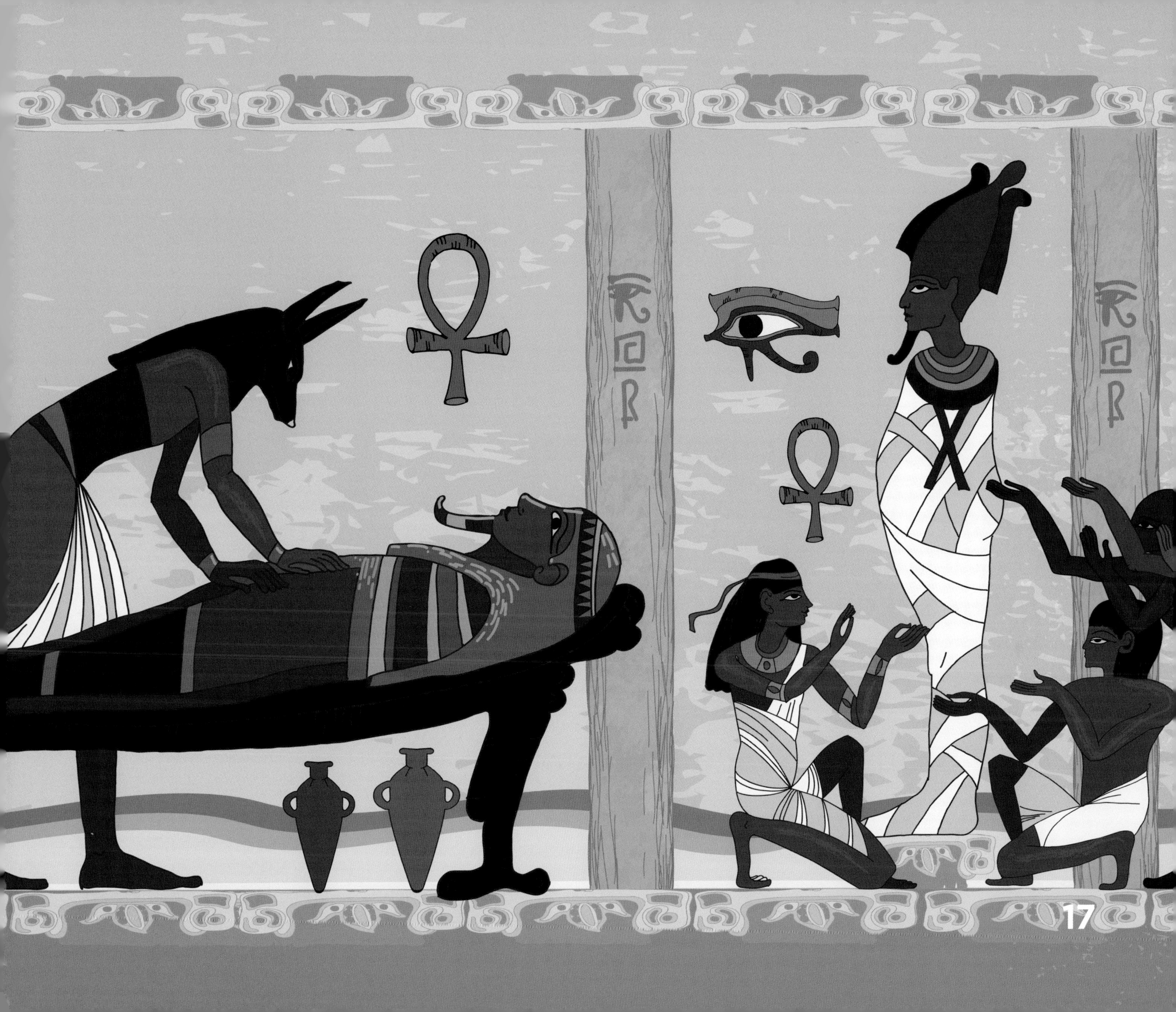

Notable Pharaohs

Hatshepsut reigned between 1478 and 1458 BCE. She was the most successful female pharaoh. She opened new routes for **trade**. She brought peace to Egypt.

Hatshepsut

19

The best-known pharaoh is King Tutankhamun, or King Tut. He took the throne in 1333 BCE at just 9 years old. He helped bring back important **traditions** to Egypt.

King Tut

More Notable Pharaohs

Khufu

Akhenaten

Cleopatra VII

c. 2575–c. 2465 BCE | 1390–1353 BCE | 1353–1336 BCE | 1279–1213 BCE | 51–30 BCE

Amenhotep III

Ramses II

Glossary

chaos – a state, condition, or place of complete confusion or disorder.

harmony – in agreement; unity.

mummify – to make a dead body into a mummy by using special chemicals and wrapping it tightly.

preserve – to protect or keep safe from loss.

temple – a place built for the official worship of the gods and in honor of Egyptian rulers.

trade – the act of exchanging or buying and selling goods.

traditions – the beliefs and customs of a group of people.

Index

Abdo Kids
ONLINE
FREE! ONLINE MULTIMEDIA RESOURCES

Visit **abdokids.com** to access crafts, games, videos, and more!

Use Abdo Kids code

DPK8466

or scan this QR code!